# Just [illegible]
# He Said



Sam Brewster

Hannah Jayne Lewin

10

The sunlight was catching the dust in the air
as some friends with a stretcher were climbing the stairs.
The crowds had spilled out from the house to the street
and were blocking the Teacher they'd travelled to meet.

As Jesus was speaking there wasn't a sound
till great chunks of the ceiling began to fall down!
To gasps of amazement a
stretcher descends,
delivered to Jesus by
four faithful friends.

A terrified paralysed man looked around

from his mat that had come to a halt on the ground.

"Your sins are forgiven,"
spoke Jesus with love,

and to show his authority
came from above

he continued, "I tell you, get up and go home!"

And to all their amazement, he got up to go!

Jesus had spoken!

The man took his bed:

From paralysed to walking,

just as he said.

Higher and higher the
waves seemed to rise

as buckets of rain fell
from tumbling skies;

gallons of water were
filling the boat,

on the thunderous sea
it was barely afloat!

Through deafening winds
came their terrified cry,

"Jesus wake up!
Don't you care if we die?"

He looked at the storm and the fear in their eyes.

He looked at the lightning that crashed from the skies.

He lifted his voice with a mighty, "Be still!"

And the weather submitted at once to his will.

The menacing skies turned a beautiful red;

from a storm to a calm,

just as he said.

Two sisters were weeping,
their brother had died,

now Jesus was with them
and all of them cried.

Could anything bring back
their brother and friend?

If only the sisters could
see him again!

"Take heart!" Jesus told them.
"Your brother will rise.

Show me the place
where Lazarus lies."

They took him, and heard him say, “Lazarus come out!”

The dead man got up at the sound of his shout,

with funeral bandages wrapped round his head;

a dead man alive,

## just as he said.

With Jerusalem only a short walk away,
Jesus was teaching his friends on the way.
"I'm going to suffer. I'm going to die.
I'll soon be rejected and lifted up high.
My blood must be shed and the price must be paid
for the sinful and lost to be found and be saved."

They looked on in horror
as Jesus was led
by a treacherous friend
to his terrible death.

He was nailed to a cross;
his disciples all fled:
Abandoned and dying,
just as he said.

But Jesus had told them this wasn't the end,
that on the third day he would rise up again.
Nobody really believed it was true
or understood what he was planning to do.

So when Jesus died his friends all forgot;
they went down with spices to hold back the rot.
But what a surprise when the stone wasn't there,
when the tomb where they laid him
was totally bare.

They looked on in shock as an angel appeared
like a floodlight of glory that filled them with fear,
and their hearts almost stopped when his thundering voice
declared with a music that filled them with joy,

"The Lord isn't here, he is raised from the dead!

He's coming to meet you,

just as he said!"

Just As He Said?

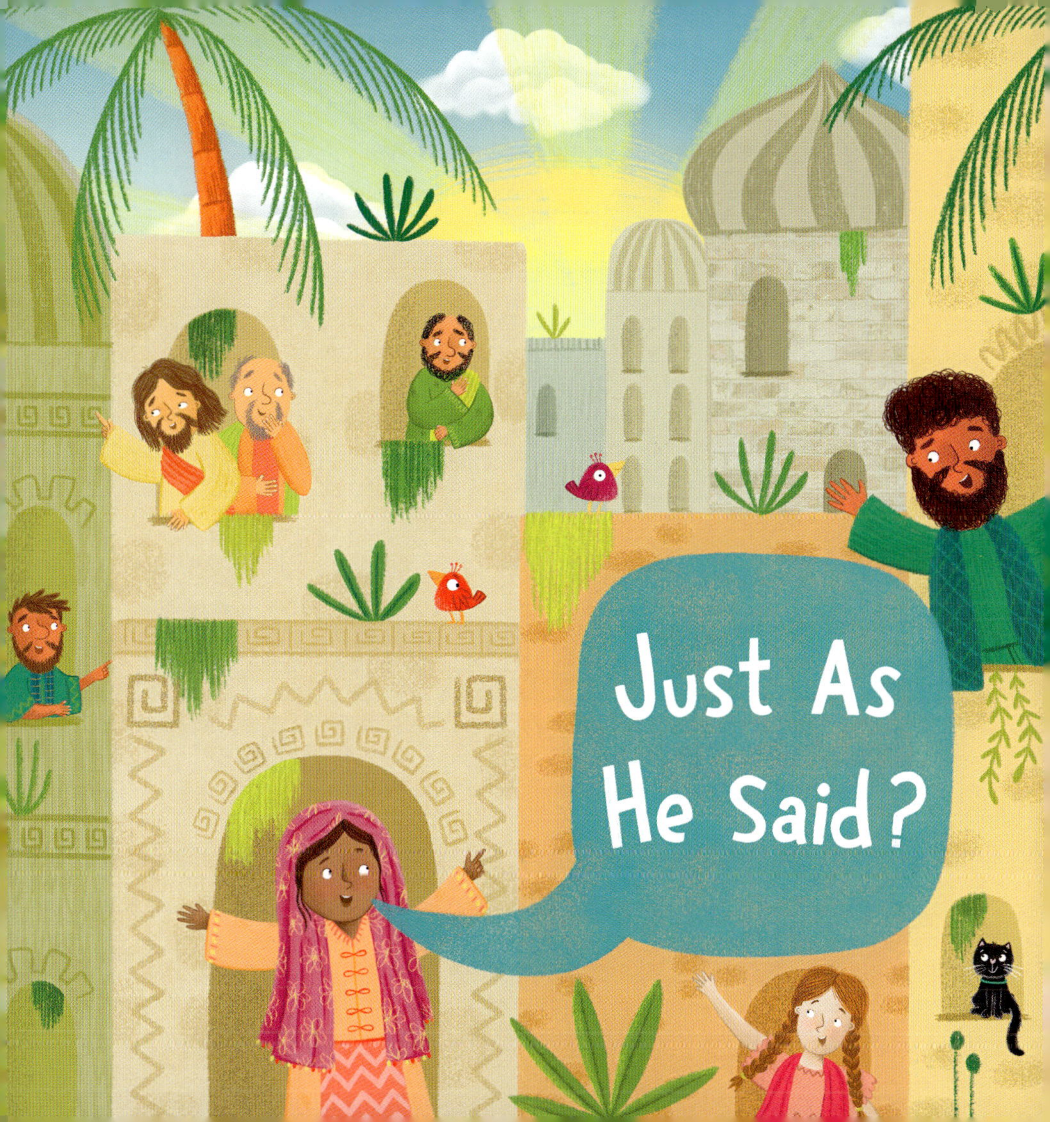
Just As He Said?

The words kept on dancing around in their heads:

All he had spoken had always come true...

They turned and they saw him. "Jesus! It's you!"

They fell down and worshipped their wonderful Lord
who'd always been faithful and true to his word,
who died for their sin, and then rose from the dead:
The conquering hero,

just as he said.

The message is simple, the message is true:

You can trust Jesus, whatever you do.

Like the paralysed man, he'll forgive all your sin
when you bring all the mess of your problems to him.
Your sin may be big but he paid it instead!
He'll completely forgive you,

just as he said.

When life is a storm and you're scared out of your mind,
he's alive and he's with you to strengthen and guide.
He's the Lord of the storm and he's walking ahead;
he'll never abandon you,

just as he said.

When death leaves you feeling confused and afraid
like the two grieving sisters that terrible day,
for those who trust Jesus there's nothing to dread:
He'll raise you up with him,

**just as he said.**

So will you trust Jesus? He calls you to come.
He calls you to trust him and all that he's done,
to trust him today and trust him tomorrow.
To trust him through days of rejoicing and sorrow,
to trust him tonight as you lie on your bed:
The Saviour who'll always do

**just as he said.**

"He is not here;
he has risen,
just as he said."

Matthew 28:6

**Sam Brewster** is Vicar of Trinity Church, Henley and author of *The Friends and the Traveller* and *The King and the Shepherd Boy*.

**Hannah Jayne Lewin** is based in Yorkshire. She is the illustrator of numerous books and her work has been highly commended for the Carmelite Prize.



British Library Cataloguing in Publication Data. A record for this book is available from the British Library.

EU GPSR: 6b Upper Water Street, Newry, Northern Ireland, BT34 1DJ.

ISBN: 978-1-83728-056-8

Designed by Diane Warnes. Printed in India.

10Publishing, a division of 10ofthose.com. Unit C, Tomlinson Road, Leyland, Lancashire, PR25 2DY.
info@10ofthose.com www.10ofthose.com

1 3 5 7 10 8 6 4 2

# More books from 10Publishing

Resources that point to Jesus

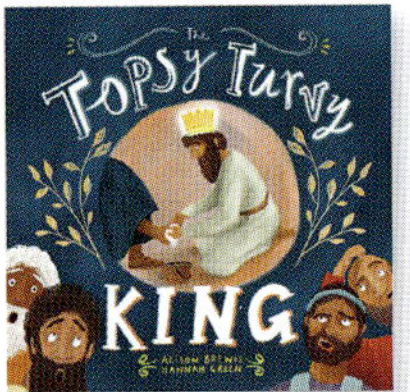

Scan here and use code ListenNow at checkout to download a free audiobook version.

10 Publishing
a division of 10 of those.com